CONTENTS

PREHISTORIC

Wood was one of the media most
readily available and convertible to
human use from earliest times. When
the first settlers, who were hunters,
arrived in Ireland some nine or ten
thousand years ago, they used wood for
the shafts of their barbs and various
flint weapons and tools. No doubt some
of their utensils were also of wood. Later, in the Neolithic period, about
3500 BC, when a more advanced society constructed the great megalithic
tombs, noteworthy for their engineering, architecture and mural art, when
the first dwelling houses were built and art pottery was made, wood must
have been used for functional and decorative purposes. Yet, apart from
wooden handles for stone axes, no wrought wood of any type has been
discovered that is datable to this vast stretch of time. This may be explained
by the very nature of wood, which is subject to decay or loss through fire. It
may also be the case that the sites at which wood is preserved have not yet
been discovered.

From about 2500 BC onwards, however, the situation begins to change,
as evidence for the use of wood becomes firmer. Round-based bowls of
willow, poplar and alder, many of which had either four or six legs, are
recorded. These were well finished and may have been polished, as was
usual during the period, and were probably used for serving food and
drink. The shapes may have been influenced by pottery vessels of the time.

Wooden boxes with lids were used to hold or store ornaments. Some
were specially shaped for gold lunulae (neck ornaments) and dress-
fasteners. One such box, dating to about 700 BC, was discovered in
Killymoon, Co Tyrone, in the early nineteenth century (Photo 1). It is
oblong or elliptical in shape and was purpose-made for the gold dress-
fastener that was found with it. Made of alder, the container part of the box
was carved from a single piece of wood, and the lid has a central
protuberance which fitted and could simply be pushed into the mouth of

Photo 1. Alder box containing a gold dress-fastener, dating to about 700 BC, discovered in Killymoon, Co Tyrone, in the early nineteenth century.

Photo 2. Block cart-wheel made of alder, with dowels of yew, dating to about 400 BC, found in a bog in Co Roscommon in 1968–9.

the hollowed-out receptacle. Not surprisingly, the piece is now warped and shrunken, and both ends are damaged.

Dug-out canoes were made from at least 2000 BC onwards, and wooden trackways were constructed from about the same date.

Carved or hollowed-out cauldrons, from the period between about 1000 BC to AD 200, are another significant group of prehistoric wooden vessels, some of which are exceptionally large. They are almost hemispherical in shape and have lug or loop handles. Their shape may have been inspired by contemporary metal cauldrons.

Small-handled wooden bowls from the period 200 BC to AD 200 mimic contemporary metal types, such as the Keshcarrigan Cup, a bronze vessel with an everted rim and a handle in the form of a bird head. Found in Keshcarrigan, Co Leitrim, it measures only about 7cm (3in) in height and was possibly used for drinking.

An important indicator of the development of wood technology is provided by two massive block cart-wheels dating to about 400 BC (Photo 2). They were found in a bog in Co Roscommon in 1968–9 and are the earliest known evidence of wheeled transport in Ireland. Each consists of three thick planks of alder fastened edge to edge with two long dowels of yew. The dowels and receivers were curved outwards from the centre, apparently to ensure that the wheel sections remained firmly in position.

EARLY CHRISTIAN

Stave-built vessels are known from the later centuries of the pre-Christian era, but the type is among the most common survivors from the first millennium AD (Photo 3). Included are tankards, buckets, tubs and casks, all sharing a fairly uniform style. A number have come from raths or crannogs, some have been discovered in bogs, and many have been found during excavations in Dublin.

Tubs and buckets are the most common type of stave-built vessel. The tubs were made in a variety of sizes. One, which measured only 145mm (5½in) in height and had a handle on one side, was almost certainly used for drinking. Others were so large that one person alone would not have been able to carry them. Such vessels would probably have been used for storing various commodities, for dyeing fabrics and for washing.

The buckets were of three main types, two large and one smaller version. The first of the larger types was made completely of wood, being bound with split wooden hoops and having a wooden swing handle. In the second type the hoops, handle and other fittings were of metal. These two types would appear to have been used for general everyday purposes. The third type of bucket was much smaller, measuring somewhere between 100mm and 200mm (4–8in) in height. While some were stave-built, most were made from a single block of wood, probably by turning (Photo 4). All of

Photo 3. Stave-built vessel bound with split wooden hoops. Early Christian/ medieval.

Photo 4. Bucket
turned from a single
piece of yew, bound
with decorative
bronze, found in
Derrymullen, Co
Laois, in 1979,
dating to about AD
800.

these smaller buckets were bound with bronze bands, which were usually decorated in openwork designs. They were generally made of yew, but oak is known to have been used in stave-built types. According to the Brehon (old Gaelic) code of law, yew was classified among the nobler trees, but its timber was declared suitable for household vessels. These small buckets may have been used to hold wine or other alcoholic drinks. They may also have been used to hold holy water, or have served some other liturgical function.

The types of utensil referred to above by no means exhaust the spectrum of wooden artefacts recorded from this period. The range includes domestic articles such as ladles, dishes, troughs, boxes and churns; craft tools such as those used in processing flax and wool; containers such as the kegs used for storing butter; toys and games. An interesting gaming board from Ballinderry, Co Westmeath, is one of the most elaborate from any site in north-west Europe during the period between the seventh and tenth centuries AD (Photo 5). The quantity of wooden artefacts from this period is so extensive and manufacturing techniques are so competently mastered as to point to the existence of professional woodworkers.

Little is known regarding prehistoric furniture, but

Photo 5. Gaming board from Ballinderry, Co Westmeath, of seventh to tenth-century date. The layout of the board would suggest that it was used for a game similar to chess or chequers.

from about the seventh century AD onwards there is evidence of beds and of free-standing benches and stools. The latter would most likely be a relative of the traditional three-legged stool which has continued in use up to the present time.

Some indications of furniture are provided by manuscript illumination and by depictions on high crosses between the eighth and tenth centuries AD. While this evidence may be considered secondary and indirect, it should be viewed as part of the contemporary ambience of achievement in the different art media. It is also strengthened by the corroboration of literary references and by the emergence in later centuries of specimens and features whose roots may be traced to these sources.

The Book of Kells which dates to about AD 800 provides some of the most interesting detail and the pieces depicted are of luxuriant quality. The very depiction of articles of furniture in these illuminations implies some confident familiarity with forms and structures, if only because the scribe or artist had to sit on some stool or chair while working at a desk or table. In contrast to metal, which at the time could be fashioned into such unrivalled masterpieces as the Ardagh Chalice or the Tara Brooch, wood in its natural state is practically ready for use and does not require any complex preparatory processing. In these circumstances therefore, it would be reasonable to deduce that, if goldsmiths and silversmiths could attain such excellence, their contemporary woodworkers could reach corresponding standards. They had certainly mastered the relevant wood technology, and the upholstery should not have presented a difficulty, as is clear from the evidence uncovered relating to tools and equipment for textile processing, for example, spindle whorls, spindles, weaving tablets and loom fragments.

In the Book of Kells, St Matthew is portrayed facing forward on a chair or throne (Pl 1). Although only the outer portions of the back and arm-supports of the throne are visible, it is clear that they form a continuous unit of arc or semicircular outline. The upholstery is brown and trimmed in gold, and the ends are decorated with diamond and rectangular patterns in red, blue and yellow.

The chair on which John the Evangelist is depicted is very similar, though it seems much smaller. The back and arm supports are richly upholstered in a blue fabric which is bound or enhanced with gilt ribbing and sweeps backward in an overhanging roll, with decorative features on the terminals. Only the ends of the supporting frame on either side of the Evangelist are visible. The legs are tapered. The frame, legs and cushion on which the Evangelist sits are all painted red/brown.

The throne or chair on which Christ is portrayed follows the same general format, but is much smaller.

The chair on which the Madonna with her Child sits is very different (Pl 2). The seat is concave and rests on legs that have spreading terminals below. The back rises above the Madonna's shoulders and terminates in an animal head. The basic colour of the chair, specifically the seat, legs and back, is yellow. The animal head is white and red. The space between the legs is enclosed, and the panel is painted with a decorative cruciform motif in red, blue and yellow, with green in the angles. The animal-head terminal is of particular interest as it is an early appearance of a feature that was to emerge later as one of the characteristics of Irish furniture.

Chairs are depicted in some of the biblical scenes on a number of high crosses. These stone crosses, which are regarded as being among the most distinctively Irish sculptural contributions, date from the ninth century onwards, while prototypes in wood date from about a century earlier. As the crosses were intended to convey messages relating to the different biblical themes represented, it is likely that the artefacts portrayed, including articles of furniture, were those that could be readily recognised.

The range of chairs represented is considerable. The backs of some are head-high, while others would barely reach the waist. In some the seats are flat, while in others they are concave or curved. The legs are clearly visible in most, but there is also evidence of enclosed or block bases. In a few instances there is evidence of upholstery.

The chairs depicted on the Moone Cross, Co Kildare (Photo 6), the Cross of Durrow, Co Offaly (Photo 7), and the Cross of Clonca, Co Donegal (Photo 8) are among the most interesting examples.

King David is represented on a number of crosses playing the lyre and harp while he sits on chairs of different types, for example, with waist-high

Photo 6. Detail from the Moone Cross, Co Kildare, depicting the sacrifice of Isaac. The chair on which Abraham sits has a high back that terminates above in an animal head. Ninth/tenth century.

Photo 7. Detail from the Cross of Durrow, Co Offaly, showing Pilate on a chair with a waist-high back and a concave seat. Ninth/tenth century.

or shoulder-high backs, concave seats and enclosed bases (Photo 9). Since the quadrilateral harp that David plays is the carved rendering of an actual instrument that was widely associated with Ireland, it should be reasonable to assume that the chair on which he sits is also representative of an actual specimen. Furthermore, the construction of a harp would be more demanding on the craftworker than would the making of a chair. The harp would have had to conform to certain musical requirements, and there could be no room for fluctuation or deviation from the norm.

8.

9.

MEDIEVAL

On the Shrine of St Maolruain's Gospel — often called the Stowe Missal — which dates to about AD 1030, a seated harper is depicted (Photo 10). The harp is quadrilateral and is probably the final representational rendering of a type that appeared frequently on the high crosses. The chair on which the harper sits also recalls earlier types, for it has a curved or concave seat that follows the body shape. This feature was first seen on the chair of the Madonna and Child in the Book of Kells, and again on a number of high crosses. By virtue of its continued use over such a long period, it would merit recognition as an accepted stylistic element. The chair on the shrine is set low and has a solid or enclosed base. The seat curves smoothly on to the back, which is about waist high. It is undecorated.

From the eleventh century onwards, extant specimens of crafted wood form a more steady sequence, but there are still gaps in the continuity. The excavations of tenth and eleventh-century sites in Dublin, which began in the early 1960s and continued for about twenty-five years, have provided evidence of woodworkers of high technical calibre. This evidence is concentrated mainly in small carved wooden artefacts. The variety is extensive and includes boxes, handles of tools, harness mounts, weavers' equipment, bowls, toggles, spoons, bench ends and chair finials. While

Photo 8. Detail from the Cross of Clonca, Co Donegal, showing a chair with a high vertical back that has a large ornamental top — probably an animal head. An armrest curves downwards from the back to connect with the front leg at seat level. This chair is unusual in that it evidently has six legs — the profile view shows three legs on one side. Ninth/tenth century.

Photo 9. Detail from the North Cross at Castledermot, Co Kildare, showing King David playing a harp as he sits on a chair with a waist-high back. Ninth/tenth century.

*Photo 10. Detail
from the Shrine of St
Maolruain's Gospel,
about AD 1030,
showing a harper on
a chair with a
concave seat.*

some of these are of tenth-century date, the bulk are from the eleventh century. With regard to furniture, the two most noteworthy pieces are a chair terminal in the form of an animal head, reflective of a feature of a chair depicted originally in the Book of Kells and later on the high crosses, decorated with an interlace motif and having traces of gilding, and a figurine that was part of a gaming set (Photo 11). In the latter, the figure sits on a cylinder-shaped stool with baluster supports that are decorated with incised trellis. The edge of the seat is lightly engraved with a band of interlace.

Figure sculptures occupy a primary position in the thirteenth and fourteenth centuries, and the carving of St Molaise from Inishmurray, Co Sligo, dating to about AD 1200, is the most noteworthy (Photo 12). The work is in oak and measures 1.5m (5ft) in height. It has been painted several times, and traces of green, red and white paint are still visible. The head, now damaged, is carved as a separate piece from the body, but the joint is hidden by the amice (hood) formation. The treatment of the ascetic features and of the different components of the dress marks this figure as a good specimen of woodcarving.

The Domhnach Airgid (literally 'silver church/shrine') provides some

11.

Photo 11. Figurine from gaming set, dating to AD 1050–1100. The figurine is seated on a cylinder-shaped stool with baluster supports that are decorated with incised trellis. The edge of the seat is lightly engraved with interlace. Excavated at Fishamble Street, Dublin.

Photo 12. Carved oak figure of St Molaise, dating to about AD 1200, from Inishmurray, Co Sligo.

indications of seat furniture about AD 1350. The original shrine, which was probably intended to hold relics, was constructed about AD 800 and was refurbished in the fourteenth and fifteenth centuries. In three different silver-gilt panels, which were added during the redecoration, Christ, the Virgin with her Child, and a bishop are shown seated. The back of the throne on which Christ sits has an ornamental trim on top, and is only about hip-high on the sitter. The base is waisted and enclosed, and is decorated in a trellis pattern (Photo 13). The Virgin's throne is similar but of smaller size (Photo 14). The bishop sits on what could more aptly be called a chair. There is a distinct top-rail with an open space underneath. The ends of the rail rest on supports that follow a concave curve downwards to form the legs (Photo 15). These three chairs have the waisted

14.   15.

format in common, i.e. the outline is narrowest at the centre, from which it curves outward in either direction. Interestingly, the core box of the Domhnach Airgid is carved from a solid block of yew and has a sliding lid.

BAROQUE

Carved wooden harps provide the main links in the progress of Irish woodworking between the fifteenth and the seventeenth centuries. These instruments are not simply the creations of a few gifted artists. As can be ascertained from the quality of the carving and from independent records relating to Irish music, they emerge from a tradition parallel to that of metalworking, where the evidence is more substantial.

The earliest of these harps is that known as the Brian Boru Harp, often referred to as the Trinity College Harp because it is preserved in Trinity College, Dublin. It dates probably to the fifteenth century, but could possibly be earlier, and is decorated all over in engraved or burned-in

Photo 14. The Virgin with her Child on a throne that has a waisted base and a hip-high back, with an ornamental trim on top. Panel from the Domhnach Airgid, dating to about AD 1350.

Photo 15. Panel from the Domhnach Airgid, dating to about AD 1350, showing a bishop on a chair that has a distinct top-rail.

patterns, most of which are geometric. Some features are of a later date, perhaps added as late as the sixteenth century.

The Cloyne Harp, made in the early seventeenth century, is arguably the most important of these unique instruments (Photo 16). It is often referred to as the Dalway Harp because it was in the possession of a Co Antrim family of the name Dalway for a considerable time. Unfortunately only the neck or harmonic curve and the forepillar now remain, the sound-box having been long lost. These two surviving parts are elaborately carved. The motifs include both natural and mythical animals, most with their names inscribed, and plants. The arms of John Fitzgerald of Cloyne, Co Cork, where the harp was made, impaled with those of his wife, Ellen Barry, are carved at the centre of the forepillar. Of great significance is a long inscription, mostly in Irish and partially in Latin, which gives the names of the maker, the harpers and various members of the Fitzgerald household. At one end of the neck is the head of a dog or wolf with open mouth, from which the remainder of the neck emerges. This feature is reminiscent of that in the twelfth-century Cross of Cong, Co Mayo, where the base of the shaft is fixed in the mouth of a double-faced animal head. At the other end of the neck is the figure of a crowned queen, holding an orb and sceptre,

Photo 16. Plaster reconstruction of the Cloyne Harp.

and, beside it, the inscription '*Ego sum regina cithararum*' meaning 'I am the queen of harps', scarcely an exaggeration for what must have been a very beautiful instrument.

The Kildare Harp, which also dates from the seventeenth century, is again richly carved and decorated (Photo 17). It originally belonged to the Fitzgeralds, Earls of Kildare, and the family arms are carved at the centre of the forepillar. The remainder of the carving includes a grotesque human mask at the lower terminal of the forepillar, an animal head — perhaps that of a wolf or dog — in high relief at the upper terminal, as well as scrolls, spirals and various geometric patterns. The appearance of the harp was enriched by colour, and traces of red, black, white, green and brown paint can still be seen.

Few articles of furniture have been preserved from the sixteenth or seventeenth centuries, even though records from the period mention a variety of elaborate pieces. These include chairs of various types and sizes, some gilt, lacquered or cushioned, and

Photo 17. The Kildare Harp, dating probably to the mid seventeenth century.

Photo 18. Oak chest inscribed:
  THE PVBLICKE CHIST OF THE COR
  PARATION OF HOZIRS & KNITERS OF ST
  GEORGES YELD NEARE DVBLIN WILIAM
  COLWORT MR IAMES PLVMLEY AND
  IAMES COCKS WARDENS 1688.

lavishly upholstered and embroidered; stools of similar range and quality to the chairs; canopied bedsteads with fine curtains or hangings; tables and cabinets (Photo 18). It is not possible to say what proportion of the articles are Irish, because imports during the period were substantial. While losses would have occurred through natural decay, the greatest destruction resulted from the ravages of war and general strife. By this time too, continental and particularly English influences had come to assert themselves on Irish furniture, and this situation was to continue (Pl 3).

EIGHTEENTH CENTURY

Photo 19. Oak cradle, about 1700.

From the early 1700s onwards, an increasing number and variety of pieces of Irish furniture have survived. Up to about the 1730s, walnut or lacquered furniture was the more fashionable, although articles made of oak were also popular (Photos 19 & 20).

cont. p 33

IRISH
FURNITURE &
WOODCRAFT

*Pl 1. Page from the
Book of Kells, about
AD 800, showing St
Matthew on a
throne that is
upholstered in
brown with gold
trim.*

*Pl 2. Page from the
Book of Kells, about
AD 800, in which
the Madonna is
shown seated with
her Child on a
painted chair. The
seat is concave while
the back rises above
the Madonna's
shoulders and
terminates in an
animal head.*

*Pl 3. (Facing page)
Gilded chair of the
Corporation of
Skinner's Alley,
1690–1700.*

*Pl 4. Mahogany
stool with apron
carved with shells
and stylised foliage,
and having cabriole
legs with trifid feet,
about 1760.*

*Pl 5. Mahogany
tray-top table with
decorative trifid feet
and shell feature on
the apron, about
1770. (Donated to
the Museum by
Ronald McDonnell.)*

*Pl 6. Mahogany
dinner-plate bucket
with brass bands
and handle, about
1780.*

*Pl 7. Carved and
painted chair, with
motifs from the
collar of the Order
of St Patrick and the
motto of the Order
of the Garter. The
figure of a dove and
'Social Club' appear
over a five-pointed
crown. Above is a
crest of wheat sheaf
over a heraldic
wreath. Late
eighteenth century.*

*Pl 8. Harp with gilt
decoration of
shamrocks and
foliage, made by
John Egan, Dublin,
about 1825.*

*Pl 9. Settle
decorated with the
arms of the four
provinces and
inscribed in old Irish
script 'Tosach
Sláinte Scíth' (Rest is
the beginning of
health) and 'Suan
na Sidhe' (The sleep
of the fairies). About
1880.*

*Pl 10. Carved yew
chair decorated with
crowned bust above
and having legs with
hoof feet. Mid
nineteenth century.*

*Pl 11. Figure of
Queen Victoria
carved in bog yew,
made by Arthur
Jones and exhibited
at the Irish
Industrial
Exhibition, Dublin,
1853.*

*Pl 12. Desk of
Killarney type,
about 1850.*

*Pl 13. Travelling
bookcase or
chiffonier by Ross of
Dublin, about
1860.*

*Pl 14. Folding card
table, about 1830.*

*Pl 15. Piano chair
by Robert Strahan,
about 1850.*

*Pl 16. (Facing page)
Cabinet by James
Hicks, Dublin,
about 1910.*

*Pl 17. Table by
James Hicks,
Dublin, about
1900.*

*Pl 18. One of a pair
of bookstands made
by Kilkenny
woodworkers, about
1910.*

cont. from p 20

A great period of Irish furniture-making was that from about 1740 to 1760, a period marked also by the most effective and widespread use of mahogany (Photo 21; Pls 4 & 5). It was during this time that Irish furniture developed the characteristics by which it is usually recognised. Generally it was of a sturdy and robust character. The aprons (decorative panels on front of or around a piece of furniture) of tables, of various sizes and types, of stools, chests and bottle stands or carriers, were carved in low relief with floral and foliate patterns, and with festoons and birds on either side of a central feature, such as a fabulous or grotesque mask, lion head, basket of flowers or scallop shell. The background to the carving was embellished by stippling or punching, or was engraved with trellis-work. Another characteristic was a protuberance above the paw or claw and ball foot. This was often decorated with stylised hair or leaves.

Not all furniture, however, was lavishly carved. Much of it was fairly plain, with an apron, for instance, carrying no more that a shell feature, or with legs having simple trifid feet or slipper-like terminals.

Photo 20. Oak chair with sunken seat to hold a cushion, dated 1726.

Mahogany staved and hooped utensils for holding turf were widely used during the eighteenth century. Some were large and tub-shaped, measuring about 60cm (23in) in height and 75cm (29in) wide, with ring handles. Others were of bucket-type, with swing or side handles.

Buckets of a similar shape and size were used to take plates to and from the diningroom and kitchen. These had part of a stave removed to provide an elongated vertical opening for the loading or unloading of plates (Pl 6).

As well as mahogany, pine was also used, and gilded pine mirror frames made around the mid eighteenth century display many characteristics of the mahogany furniture, flowers. Others, in addition, houses, while others still designs.

Towards the end of Irish furniture was of a reflecting classical influences of pieces and in the ornaments), urns and decoration (Pl 7). It had, of its distinctive elements.

such as masks or baskets of depict animals and exotic follow purely architectural

the eighteenth century, more delicate construction in the elliptical shapes paterae (shallow saucer-like festoons depicted in the however, lost most if not all

Photo 22. Guitar by William Gibson, 6 Grafton Street, Dublin, 1778.

NINETEENTH CENTURY

Although much painted furniture was in use during the early years of the nineteenth century, it is the treatment of harps that is most readily recognisable as Irish. They were made in two sizes, the smaller having the wider colour range, being painted in green, black, light brown or cream, with a profusion of shamrock patterns, usually in gold (Pl 8).

In the nineteenth century three uniquely Irish types of furniture and woodcraft were developed. These were (a) the neo-Celtic style, (b) the bog-wood furniture, and (c) the Killarney types. All three were, to a degree, interrelated, and shared a common inspiration.

The neo-Celtic style

From the late eighteenth century, there was an emerging consciousness of national identity, which became even greater during the nineteenth century. With it came a growing interest in Irish antiquities and cultural achievements, and this was enlivened by various scholarly publications of historical research. It was given additional impetus, approval and confirmation by the accidental discovery of some of the greatest Irish art treasures, including the Tara Brooch. The result was the development of a style of art that can now be recognised as neo-Celtic because it revived forms and motifs from early Irish art. It began to emerge about the 1840s and continued in varying ways until modern times. The impact was to be seen across the whole art spectrum, initially in metalwork and later in woodwork, where its expression was confined almost entirely to decoration. The intrinsic feature of the style was interlacing in various forms. Numerous articles of furniture, including chairs, settles and cabinets, were carved, engraved or painted with interlaced patterns (Pl 9).

In the late nineteenth century the Arts and Crafts movement, which was interested in handicrafts and design, gave neo-Celticism a new boost. Within the movement, Irish art from the early Christian period was held in high regard, for it was considered to embody a national style and character. The belief was also expressed that the early work should not simply be copied, but should be studied and analysed so as to encourage the emergence of a new art form.

*Photo 23. Chair
painted in neo-
Celtic style, about
1910.*

Bog-wood furniture

From as early as the seventeenth century, quality furniture was made from the stumps and trunks of ancient trees, including oak, fir and yew, that had lain buried but preserved in bogs. It was probably during the nineteenth century that bog-wood was most widely used for a great range of purposes. Yew was thought to resemble rosewood, but to be superior to it in the beauty of its colour and in its texture and firmness. It was also very durable (Pl 10). Bog oak was said to become black when exposed to the air and was valued for its great strength and hardness. While bog-wood was competently worked by many manufacturers, Arthur Jones, who operated from 1820 to 1860 in Dublin, is probably the most closely associated with it, particularly with the manufacture of bog yew furniture, in which he specialised (Pl 11). He was best known for what he described as 'a suite of sculptured decorative furniture', which comprised a cabriolet sofa, occasional side-table, semi-circular side-table, whist table, card table ('loo' table), lady's work table, teapoy (small table or tripod), omnium (shelved stand for ornaments), stand for a time-piece, pair of pole firescreens, armchair, sarcophagus wine cooler, music temple (decorative cabinet celebrating musical themes) and other pieces. The design was ambitious and elaborate, aimed at illustrating subjects from early Irish history, specifically antiquities, legends, monarchs and animals, and depicting the harp, the shamrock and the wolfhound, which were common Irish emblems.

Apart from Jones, there were many other manufacturers of fine bog-wood furniture in various parts of the country. Among them were Curran of Lisburn, Bell and McCormick of Belfast, Egan of Killarney, and Fletcher of Cork. Furthermore, some manufacturers used ordinary timber to make furniture in the historic mode, relating the decoration to themes from earlier times.

Bog-wood, particularly fir and oak, was also used for making furniture of a more modest and less expensive type, which would now be classified as 'folk' or 'vernacular'. In this category came articles such as beds, chairs, stools, dressers and spinning wheels.

From the 1820s for about a century, bog oak was also used for the manufacture of small articles, intended mainly for the tourist or souvenir trade, reaching a peak from about 1850 to 1860. The range of products was amazingly diverse, extending from the simple to the elaborate, often carved, or embellished with gold, silver or gems. In general they comprised three main categories: (a) personal or dress ornaments, e.g. brooches (many similar in form to the Tara Brooch), bracelets, earrings, buttons and studs, some being in the form of or depicting shamrocks or harps, (b) household ornaments, e.g. models or representations of Irish antiquities, monuments or natural features, such as the ancient Irish harp, various abbeys or the Giant's Causeway, miniatures or caricatures of historical Irish personalities, for example Henry Grattan and Brian Boru, or even the stage Irishman, and (c) functional articles, e.g. work boxes, card cases, book stands, candlesticks and candelabra.

The shamrock was the most common decorative motif, being carved on most of the objects.

Killarney woodcraft

From the early nineteenth century until the mid twentieth century, distinctive types of articles were made in Killarney and at the Gap of Dunloe, approximately 9.5km (6 miles) from Killarney town. The articles are distinctive primarily because of the use of arbutus, a whitish close-grained wood that yellows with age. Arbutus had been highly valued from early times, and was referred to in the section on tree-damage in the Seanchas Mór (literally 'Great Tradition'), the most important collection of old Irish law texts. The Seanchas Mór mainly relates to the northern midlands, and it is likely to have been put together in a law school in that region. It is significant therefore that it should express concern for a tree that was unlikely to survive outside the south-west.

Killarney woodwork is easily recognisable in that it is all inlaid with combinations of elements from a range of motifs. These include local ruins and other well-known or historic buildings, for example Muckross Abbey, Ross Castle, Muckross House or Glena Cottage (Pl 12). Of these, Muckross Abbey was the most popular, and in consequence the artefacts were often referred to as Muckross Abbey work. National symbols also

*Photo 24. Table of
Killarney type, mid
nineteenth century.*

*Photo 25. (Facing
page) Cabinet of
Killarney type, mid
nineteenth century.*

feature, for example the harp and the rose, thistle and shamrock. The shamrock assumed a dominant position, being used profusely in borders and appearing, as far as can be seen, on every Killarney piece. Ivy leaves seem to have replaced the rose, thistle and shamrock on later pieces. Local flora, almost exclusively berried sprays of arbutus, fern, acorns and oak leaves, are another common motif.

The range of articles made extended from large pieces of furniture, intended for domestic use, to small, easily transportable articles, intended mainly for the tourist or souvenir market. Included were circular, elliptical or wavy-edged pedestal tables, measuring between about 120cm (47in) and 150cm (59in) in diameter, writing desks, cabinets, work tables, 'loo' or card tables, book stands, writing boxes, and work boxes in great variety (Photos 24 & 25). The woods used were all local — specifically maple, sycamore, yew, holly and, above all, arbutus.

Interestingly, Arthur Jones of Dublin also made furniture of the
Killarney type.

Travel furniture

Furniture that could easily be dismantled or folded, packed and
reassembled, became popular during the late eighteenth century and
continued to be made throughout most of the 1800s. Suites specially made
for army or navy officers might include bedsteads, tables, chairs, stools,
bookcases or chiffoniers, desks and, probably the best-known articles,
military chests. Ross of Dublin was an important maker of travel furniture
(Pl 13). He started business in 1821 under the title 'Army Furniture
Warehouse' and his firm continued in operation throughout the century.
He was a main supplier of furniture to officers of the British Army in India,
and this is not surprising given that many of them were Irish. One of his
most important suites, made in 1863, was a wedding present for a Captain
and Mrs Simner of Dublin, before their departure for India. It consisted of
a dining table, chairs, sideboard and sofa.

Travel furniture was not, however, made exclusively for army purposes.
There was also a market for it among wealthier emigrants who could use it
aboard ship and in their new homes in their adopted countries.

Baroque and classical styles

In addition to the distinctive woodcraft and furniture described above, fine
quality furniture in the baroque and classical modes continued to be made
in Ireland throughout the nineteenth century (Pl 14).

Some of the better-known makers were: the Del Vecchios, who were of
Italian stock but who settled in Dublin — some of their tables recall
features on Irish furniture around the mid eighteenth century; Mack
Williams and Gibton, described as 'Upholders to His Majesty's Board of
Works', who made many fine pieces in mahogany and rosewood; Strahan,
who drew on various European models (Photo 26; Pl 15); Butler, whose
firm specialised in reproducing Irish eighteenth-century mahogany
furniture; James Hicks, whose working period spanned the late nineteenth
and early twentieth centuries and who described himself as a collector,

restorer and cabinet-maker (Pls 16 & 17). Hicks is accepted as the best of his time, being among the great Irish makers.

Photo 26. Table by Robert Strahan, about 1860.

MODERN

As the twentieth century progressed, the concept of design was gradually given greater recognition. This was heralded primarily by the work of three talented, avant-garde architect-designers: Eileen Gray, Frederick MacManus and Raymond McGrath.

Eileen Gray (1879–1976) was born in Enniscorthy, Co Wexford, but spent most of her life in Paris. She attained an international reputation and fame for the furniture she designed, and which she had made by her own craftworkers.

Frederick MacManus (1903–1985) was born in Dublin, where he undertook his early architectural studies. In 1924 he moved to London to continue his studies, and lived there for most of his life. He received numerous honours or awards for architectural work, but he also designed interiors and furniture.

Raymond McGrath (1903–1977) studied in Australia in the early twenties and undertook further study in England after 1926. About 1930 he designed a range of furniture (Photo 27), and during the decade that followed he also carried out some major interior design work in London and Manchester. In 1940 he was appointed architect to the Office of Public Works in Dublin, becoming principal architect for the period 1948–68.

An agency that had a very significant impact on design was the Kilkenny Design Workshop. It came into existence in 1963 as a result of initiatives

Photo 27 (a & b). Table and chair designed by Raymond McGrath, about 1930. Donated to the Museum by Jenny O'Donovan.

a

b

by An Córas Tráchtála (The Irish Export Board) to improve standards of industrial design. The emphasis initially was on craft-based industries and on the revival of craft skills. In its wood-turning workshop, for instance, many craftworkers were trained (a number of whom later set up their own businesses) and the exploration of the potential of native timbers, including bog oak, was encouraged. Since the main aim of Kilkenny Design was to develop product ranges suitable for multiple production, the promotion of handicrafts, concentrating on the manufacture of unique artefacts, did not come within its scope.

Responsibility in that particular area was assumed by the Crafts Council of Ireland, which Kilkenny Design helped to found in 1977. The basic function of the Council is to foster the development of the craft sector by encouraging the attainment of the highest standards. With promotion from the Council, there has in recent years been a revival of the design and manufacture of furniture and of wood artefacts generally, with special emphasis on the use of native timbers. At the same time both public and private bodies have provided designer-craftworkers with lucrative opportunities, the most prestigious of which were the furnishing of Dublin Castle and of Government Buildings (formerly the College of Science) in Merrion Street.

A most significant development was the establishment of The Furniture College in Letterfrack, Co Galway, in 1987, providing a course in design and manufacture for students from all over Ireland. The college's aim is to provide a base for the continuation and development of a quality Irish furniture industry and to enable its graduates to contribute to, and influence, the design and manufacture of modern furniture in ways that are creative and responsive to social and economic needs. It seeks also to provide the seed ground for the development of an indigenous approach to furniture-making and to enhance the influence of Irish furniture design in the marketplace. Current plans are well advanced for the development of further education and training initiatives that will support the Irish furniture industry well into the next century.